Rookie

Read-About® Health

Cuts and Scrapes

By Sharon Gordon

Consultants

Nanci R. Vargus, Ed.D.
Primary Multiage Teacher
Decatur Township Schools, Indianapolis, Indiana

Jayne L. Waddell, R.N., M.A., L.P.C.
School Nurse, Health Educator, Lic. Professional Counselor

ᏅᏝ Children's Press®
A Division of Scholastic Inc.
New York   Toronto   London   Auckland   Sydney
Mexico City   New Delhi   Hong Kong
Danbury, Connecticut

Designer: Herman Adler Design
Photo Researcher: Caroline Anderson
The photo on the cover shows a girl looking at a scrape on a boy's knee.

Library of Congress Cataloging–in–Publication Data

Gordon, Sharon.
    Cuts and scrapes / by Sharon Gordon; consultants Nanci R. Vargus...
[et al.].
        p. cm. — (Rookie read-about health)
    Includes index.
    Summary: Explains what cuts and scrapes are, how they heal, and how
they should be treated.
    ISBN 0-516-22566-9 (lib. bdg.)   0-516-26870-8 (pbk.)
    1. Wound healing—Juvenile literature. [1. Wounds and injuries.
2. Wound healing. 3. First aid.] I. Title. II. Series.
RD93. G675   2002
617.1—dc21

                                        2001002691

Riding a bike is fun!

Falling down is not.

Ouch! It hurts when you scrape your knees.

5

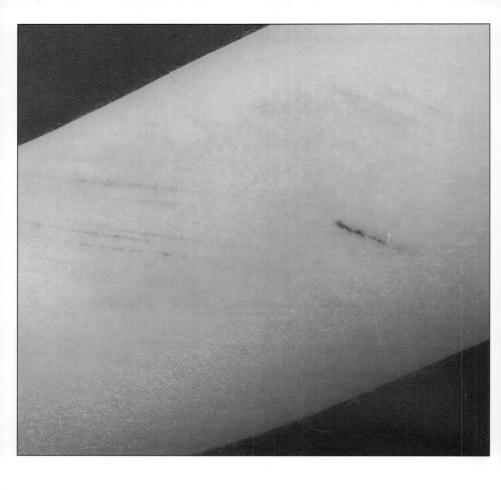

Cuts and scrapes are
breaks in the skin.

A cut is deeper than a scrape. It takes longer to heal, or get better.

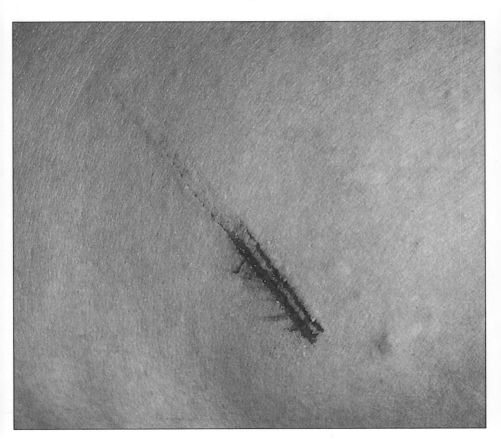

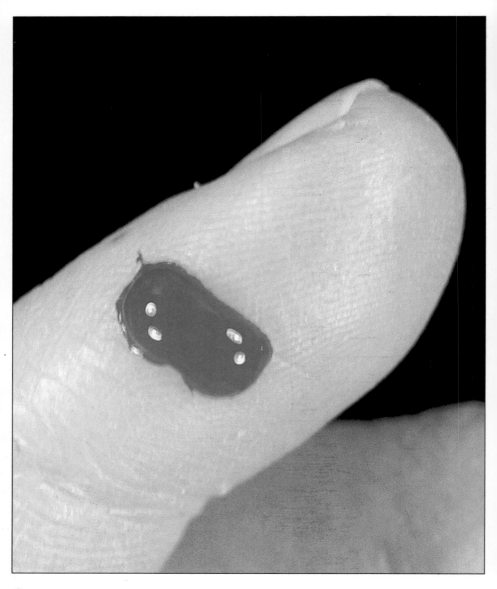

8

Your skin starts to bleed
when it is cut.

But do not be afraid.

Blood is just what your
cut needs!

Your blood is made up
of many tiny parts called
cells (sels).

Most cells are red, like
the color of your blood.

This is what red cells
look like under a
powerful microscope
(MYE-kruh-skope).

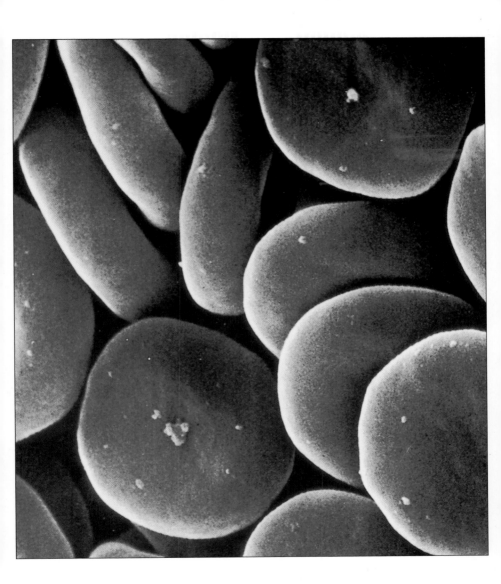

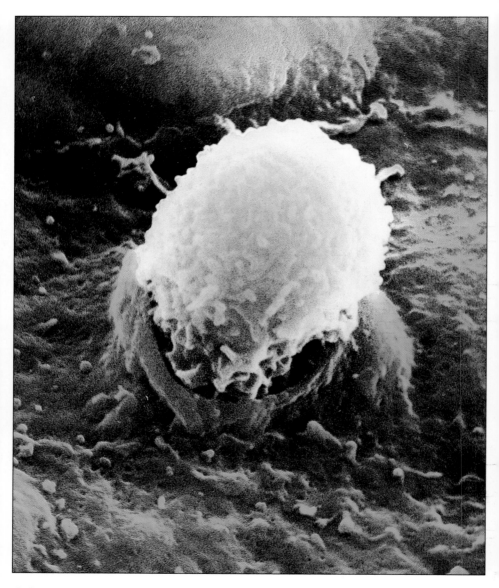

12

Other cells are white. The white cells fight the germs that get into your cut.

This is what a white cell looks like under a powerful microscope.

Your blood also has special cells called platelets (PLATE-lits). They get right to work when you get a cut or scrape!

This is what platelets look like under a powerful microscope.

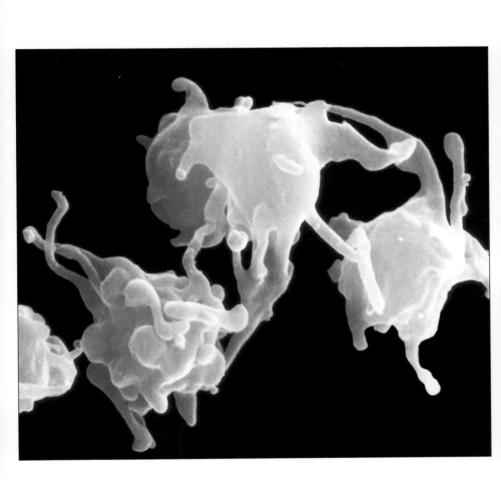

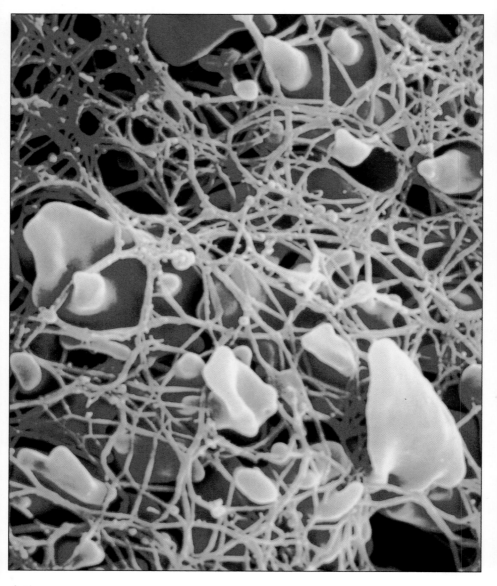

16

Many of these platelets travel quickly to the cut. They stick together in a clump. They plug up the cut.

This is what a clump of platelets would look like under a powerful microscope.

This clump of platelets
stops the bleeding. Then
the clump becomes hard.
It turns into a scab.

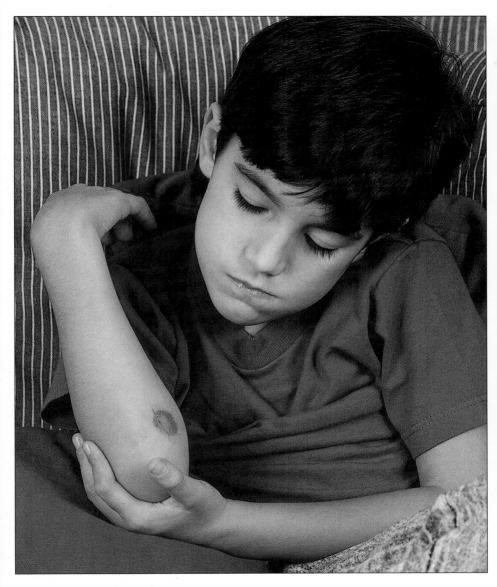

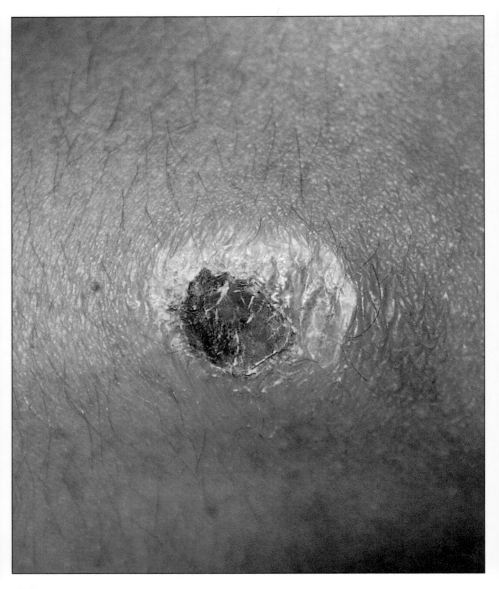

20

New skin is made under the scab.

The scab falls off when the skin is ready.

That is amazing!

Always show an adult
your cuts and scrapes.

You must wash them
with lots of soap and
water. Then put first–aid
ointment (OINT-muhnt)
on the cuts or scrapes.

A bandage will help
keep them clean.

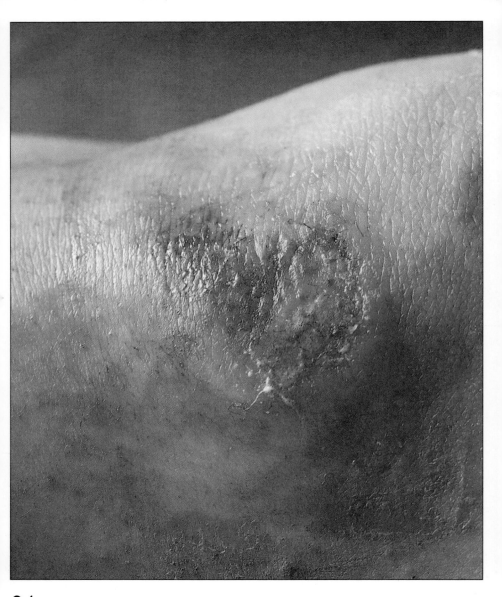

24

Your cut can get infected if you do not keep it clean.

It will get red and puffy. It might hurt when you touch it.

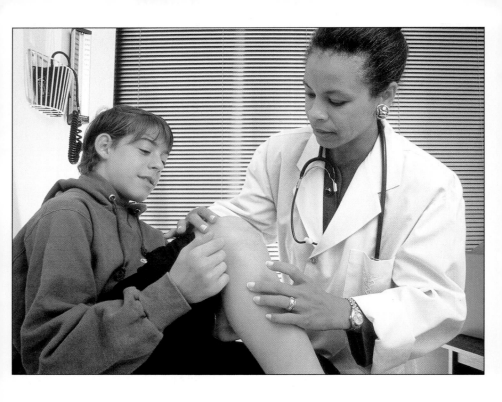

You might have to see a
doctor if a cut is really deep.
Sometimes, a few stitches
help it heal faster.

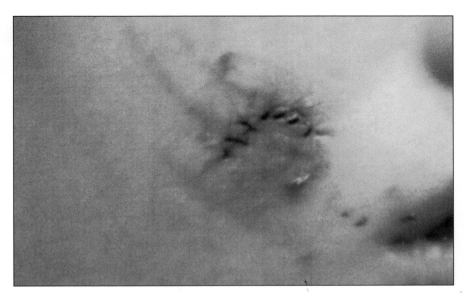

Remember, your job is to keep your cuts and scrapes clean.

Your amazing skin will do the rest!

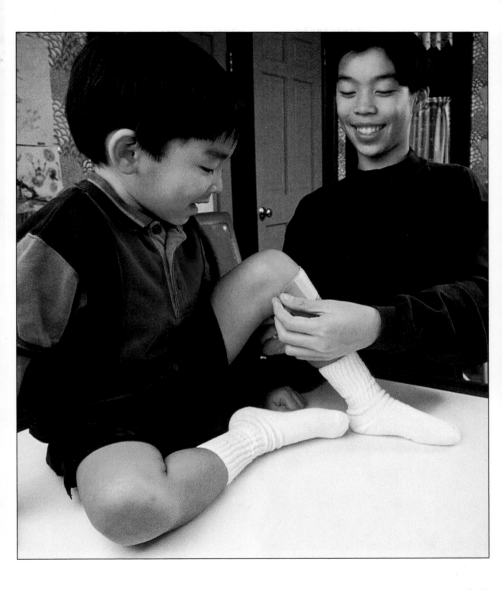

Words You Know

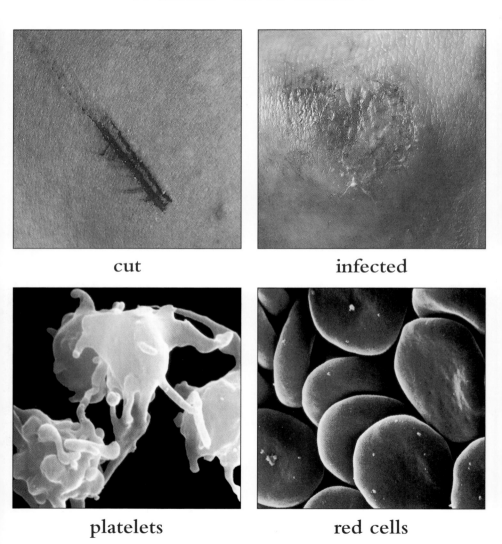

cut

infected

platelets

red cells

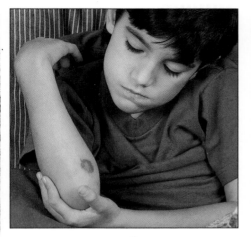

scab

scrape

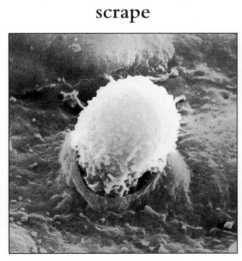

stitches

white cell

31

Index

About the Author

Sharon Gordon is a writer living in Midland Park, New Jersey. She and her husband have three school-aged children and a spoiled pooch. Together they enjoy visiting the Outer Banks of North Carolina as often as possible.

Photo Credits